Texts *for* Sh

GW01454186

Chosen by John Foster and

Contents

OXFORD
UNIVERSITY PRESS

The Pudding Like a Night on the Sea

'I'm going to make something special for your mother,' my father said.

My mother was out shopping. My father was in the kitchen looking at the pots and the pans and the jars of this and that.

'What are you going to make?' I said.

'A pudding,' he said.

My father is a big man with wild black hair. When he laughs, the sun laughs in the window-panes. When he thinks, you can almost see his thoughts sitting on all the tables and chairs. When he is angry, me and my little brother Huey shiver to the bottom of our shoes.

'What kind of pudding will you make?' Huey said.

'A wonderful pudding,' my father said. 'It will taste like a whole raft of lemons. It will taste like a night on the sea.'

Then he took down a knife and sliced five lemons in half. He squeezed the first one. Juice squirted in my eye.

'Stand back!' he said, and squeezed again. The seeds flew out on the floor. 'Pick up those seeds, Huey!' he said.

Huey took the broom and swept them up.

My father cracked some eggs and put the yolks in a pan and the whites in a bowl. He rolled up his sleeves and pushed back his hair and beat up the yolks. 'Sugar, Julian!' he said, and I poured in the sugar.

'He went on beating. Then he put in lemon juice and cream and set the pan on the stove. The pudding bubbled and he stirred it fast. Cream splashed on the stove.

'Wipe that up, Huey!' he said.

Huey did.

It was hot by the stove. My father loosened his collar and pushed at his sleeves. The stuff in the pan was getting thicker and thicker. He held the beater up high in the air. 'Just right!' he said, and sniffed in the smell of the pudding.

He whipped the egg whites and mixed them into the pudding. The pudding looked softer and lighter than air.

'Done!' he said. He washed all the pots, splashing water on the floor, and wiped the counter so fast his hair made circles around his head.

'Perfect!' he said. 'Now I'm going to take a nap. If something important happens, bother me. If nothing important happens, don't bother me. And – the pudding is for your mother. Leave the pudding alone!'

He went to the living room and was asleep in a minute, sitting straight up in his chair.

Huey and I guarded the pudding.

'Oh, it's a wonderful pudding,' Huey said.

'With waves on the top like the ocean,' I said.

'I wonder how it tastes,' Huey said.

'Leave the pudding alone,' I said.

'If I just put my finger in – then I'll know how it tastes,' Huey said.

And he did it.

'You did it!' I said. 'How does it taste?'

'It tastes like a whole raft of lemons,' he said. 'It tastes like a night on the sea.'

'You've made a hole in the pudding!' I said. 'But since you did it, I'll have a taste.' And it tasted like a whole night of lemons. It tasted like floating at sea.

'It's such a big pudding,' Huey said. 'It can't hurt to have a little more.'

'Since you took more, I'll have more,' I said.

'That was a bigger lick than I took!' Huey said. 'I'm going to have more again.'

'Whoops!' I said.

'You put in your whole hand!' Huey said. 'Look at the pudding you spilled on the floor!'

'I am going to clean it up,' I said. And I took the rag from the sink.

'That's not really clean,' Huey said.

'It's the best I can do,' I said.

'Look at the pudding!' Huey said.

It looked like craters on the moon.

'We have to smooth this over,' I said. 'So it looks the way it did before! Let's get spoons.'

And we evened the top of the pudding with spoons, and while we evened it, we ate some more.

'There isn't much left,' I said.

'We were supposed to leave the pudding alone,' Huey said.

'We'd better get away from here,' I said. We ran into our bedroom and crawled under the bed. After a long time we heard my father's voice.

'Come into the kitchen, dear,' he said. 'I have something for you.'

'Why, what is it?' my mother said, out in the kitchen.

Under the bed, Huey and I pressed ourselves to the wall.

'Look,' said my father, out in the kitchen. 'A wonderful pudding.'

'Where is the pudding?' my mother said.

'Where are you boys?' my father said. His voice went through every crack and corner of the house.

We felt like two leaves in a storm.

'Where are you, I said!' My father's voice was booming.

Huey whispered to me, 'I'm scared.'

We heard my father walking slowly through the rooms.

'Huey!' he called. 'Julian!'

We could see his feet. He was coming into our room.

He lifted the bedspread. There was his face, and his eyes like black lightning. He grabbed us by the legs and pulled.

'Stand up!' he said.

We stood.

'What do you have to tell me?' he said.

'We went outside,' Huey said, 'and when we came back, the pudding was gone!'

'Then why were you hiding under the bed?' my father said.

We didn't say anything. We looked at the floor.

'I can tell you one thing,' he said. 'There is going to be some beating here now! There is going to be some whipping!'

The curtains at the window were shaking. Huey was holding my hand.

'Go into the kitchen!' my father said. 'Right now!'

We went into the kitchen.

'Come here, Huey!' my father said.

Huey walked towards him, his hands behind his back.

'See these eggs?' my father said. He cracked them and put the yolks in a pan and set the pan on the counter. He stood a chair by the counter.

'Stand up there,' he said to Huey.

Huey stood on the chair by the counter.

'Now it's time for your beating!' my father said.

Huey started to cry. His tears fell in with the egg yolks.

'Take this!' my father said. My father handed him the egg beater. 'Now beat those eggs,' he said. 'I want this to be a good beating!'

'Oh!' Huey said. He stopped crying. And he beat the egg yolks.

'Now you, Julian, stand here!' my father said.

I stood on a chair by the table.

'I hope you're ready for your whipping!'

I didn't answer. I was afraid to say yes or no.

'Here!' he said, and he set the egg whites in front of me. 'I want these whipped and whipped well!'

'Yes, sir!' I said, and started whipping.

My father watched us, My mother came into the kitchen and watched us.

After a while Huey said, 'This is hard work.'

'That's too bad,' my father said. 'Your beating's not done!' And he added sugar and cream and lemon

juice to Huey's pan and put the pan on the stove. And
Huey went on beating.

'My arm hurts from whipping,' I said.

'That's too bad,' my father said. 'Your whipping's
not done.'

So I whipped and whipped, and Huey beat and
beat.

'Hold that beater in the air, Huey!' my father said.

Huey held it in the air.

'See!' my father said. 'A good pudding stays on the beater. It's thick enough now. Your beating's done.' Then he turned to me. 'Let's see those egg whites, Julian!' he said. They were puffed up and fluffy. 'Congratulations, Julian!' he said. 'Your whipping's done.'

He mixed the egg whites into the pudding himself. Then he passed the pudding to my mother.

'A wonderful pudding,' she said. 'Would you like some, boys?'

'No, thank you,' we said.

She picked up a spoon. 'Why, this tastes like a whole raft of lemons,' she said. 'This tastes like a night on the sea.'

Ann Cameron

On a Wet Sunday

A play with two characters:
a dad and a daughter

Dad	Stop fidgeting will you! Why don't you go upstairs and read a book or something?
Daughter	No, I've got nothing to read. What can I do?
Dad	Why don't you get the playing cards from the drawer in the kitchen and we'll play Patience or Switch or Snap or something. We could do some card tricks.
Daughter	No.
Dad	Why not?
Daughter	Don't want to.
Dad	Why don't you go to Sam's house and play with her?
Daughter	She's gone to her swimming lessons. What can I do?

Dad   Well, why don't you go upstairs, fill your brother's wellies with tomato sauce, then eat the soap in the bathroom, pour yesterday's soup all over your sister's bed, paint the walls pink and all the carpets yellow, bore holes in all the doors, flood the toilet, put all your mother's best books in the washing machine and switch it to 'rinse', empty the Hoover dustbag into your sister's tights, rip up all my poems, then squirt toothpaste all over the bathroom windows!

Daughter   No.

Dad   Huh! That's all too boring for you, I suppose.

Daughter   No. It's just that I did all that ten minutes ago.

John Rice

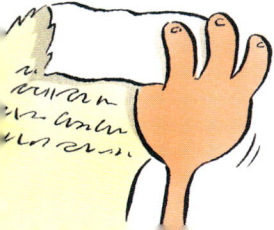

13

Seahorses

Waves
and breakers
tumbling ✱ rippling
across the sea,
smash them-
selves to
pieces, on
the shore,
in front of me.
When angry tempests
blow, wild horses
out of reach, plunge   and
toss snowy heads   and race
towards the beach.   White
crested seahorses,
prancing towards
the land. Each
striving to
be first to
collapse
upon the
strand.
Seahor-
ses,
sea-
hor-
ses,
white
breakers
on the
sand.   *Janis Priestly*

Pants

the wind came roar
ing from the sea
it reeled around
respectable trees
it jigged   the roof
tiles up   and down
and knoc   ked old
ladies   to the
ground   …but
worst,   in its
rough   panting
play   it dan
ced my   clean
pants   clean
away

Dave Calder

Orange

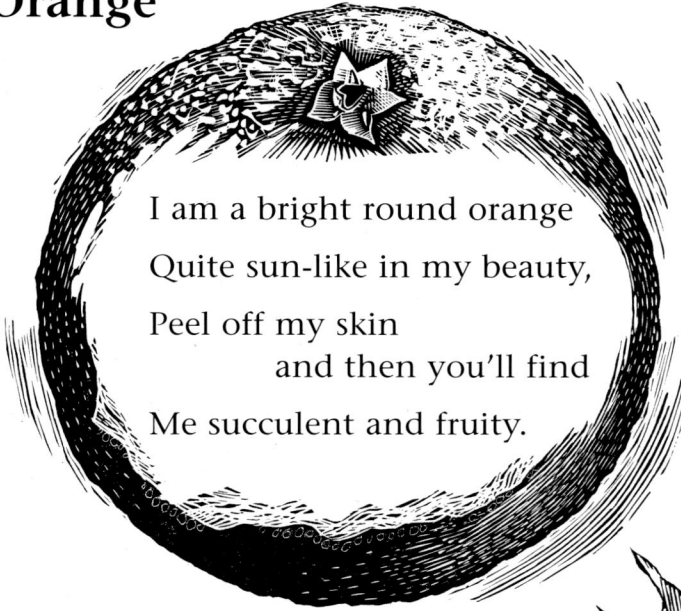

I am a bright round orange
Quite sun-like in my beauty,
Peel off my skin
      and then you'll find
Me succulent and fruity.

John Cotton

Pineapple

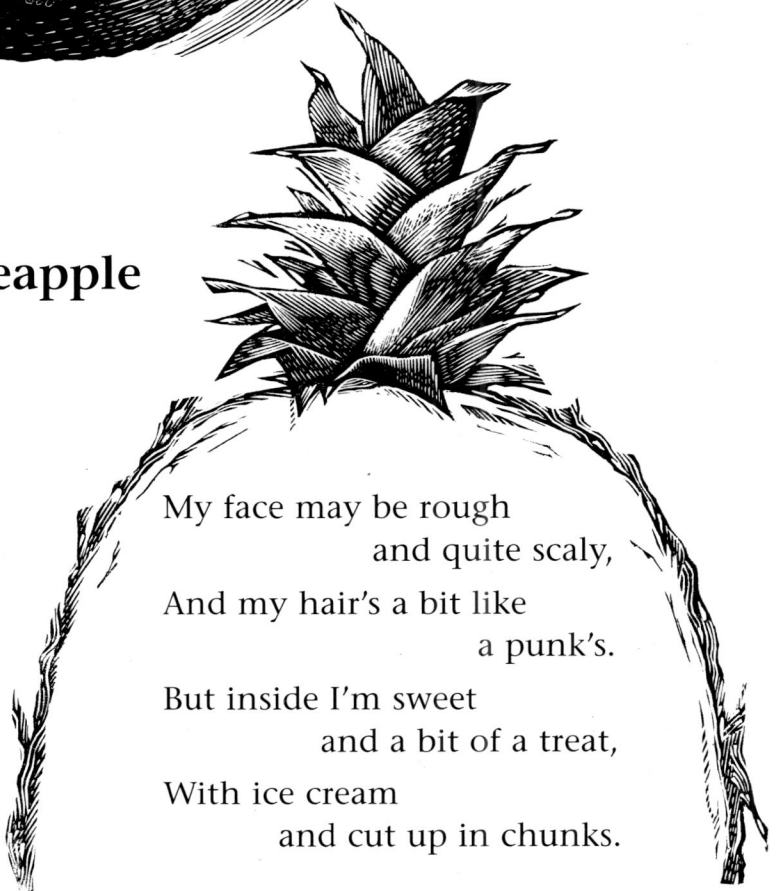

My face may be rough
      and quite scaly,
And my hair's a bit like
      a punk's.
But inside I'm sweet
      and a bit of a treat,
With ice cream
      and cut up in chunks.

John Cotton

Fun with Lists

Ten words which are fun to say...

bamboozle
dodo
flip-flop
cacomistle
poppycock
peapod
pimple
shillyshally
pterodactyl
WHIZZ!

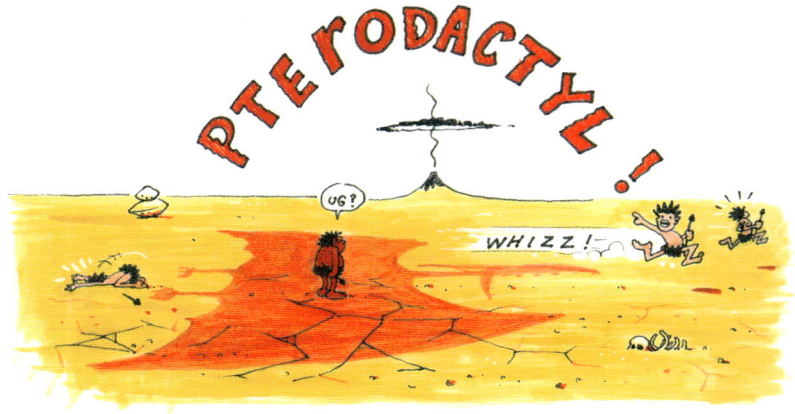

(Further choices: giggle, hobbledehoy, hoi-polloi, skulduggery, lollipop, snivel, gobbledygook, thingummajig...)

Ten beautiful words...

murmuring
lingering
lonely
windblown
rain-washed
sighing
rosemary
swallowtail
firefly
lush

(Extras: waver, golden, wanderer, drift, lull, dewberry, speckled, dragonfly, whispering, misty, rosebay willow herb... last one's a slight cheat!)

Eleven words to use instead of said...

mumble
grumble
mutter
drone
grunt
stutter
yell
moan
snivel
groan
squeal

Ten things to eat beginning with G...

grape
greengage
groundnut
gooseberry pie
gravy
garlic ice-cream*
ginger biscuit
goulash
Granny Smith apple
Garibaldi biscuit

* They make it in California, honestly!

Judith Nicholls

The Giant Awakes

It was like an earthquake. The giant was waking up after his long sleep. It had been a very long sleep, since someone of such extraordinary size needed an extraordinarily long sleep – years in fact. He shook the birds out of his long curly hair where they had perched as if on the twigs of trees. He sneezed and blew the rabbits out of his nostrils where they had been sheltering. During his very long sleep seeds had rooted where the wind had blown dust into the creases in his clothes. When he stretched himself whole gardens of flowers slithered down his sides. Bats that had been hanging from the linings of his pockets flew away in alarm.

When he stood up the fox that had climbed onto the toecap of his left boot had to jump to safety.

The giant slowly walked away from his resting place, leaving a deep, wide hollow where his enormous weight had pressed down the ground. Next time it rained, water collected in the hollow, and every time it rained the water that had gathered grew deeper and wider till it became a lake. People who rowed their boats across it named it after the giant who once slept there – Maximus Lake.

Stanley Cook

Surprise-Your-Mum-Mocha-Chocca-Trifle

This trifle is incredibly impressive, nobody will believe you've made it yourself!

To make it you need:

Two chocolate swiss rolls
Two packets of Chocolate Angel Delight
One packet of Dream Topping
Three quarters to one pint of milk
Three teaspoons instant coffee
Mug of hot water
Whipped cream for decoration
Chocolate Flake for decoration

A mixing bowl
A mug
A whisk or electric mixer
A large spoon
A trifle dish, large
(This pudding is so delicious you always want to make a lot of it!)

First of all, break the swiss rolls into quite small pieces and place them in the bottom of the trifle dish.

Put the instant coffee into the mug of hot water and stir until it's dissolved.

Pour the coffee over the swiss rolls. Leave to cool.

Empty into the mixing bowl the two packets of Angel Delight and the packet of Dream Topping. Pour about three quarters of a pint of milk into it and whisk. Leave it to set for two or three minutes and then test the mixture. It should be like a mousse, firm but soft. If it's not soft enough, add some more milk and whisk again.

Pile the mixture on top of the cooled swiss roll. Decorate with whipped cream, crushed chocolate flake and anything else you fancy.

You can cool this trifle in the fridge for an hour if you wish, but it should be eaten as soon as possible before the chocolate mixture 'collapses'.

Serve with a smile on your face and stand back because people will **rush** for it, it is so good. Make sure you get a dishful for yourself!

Irene Yates

Steg-in-the-Dumps

Poor Stegosaurus,
He's lonely and sad.
There's no one to play
And the weather's all bad.
He's sick of the rain,
And the mists of the swamp.
He wishes he wasn't
Too clumsy to romp.
It's not asking much
To be playful and slim –
But he's such an odd shape
That he can't even swim!
He's hefty and huge
And his tail weighs a ton,
So running and jumping
Poor Steg's never done!

The plates on his back
Are a terrible bind.
And he's only a walnut-sized
Brain for a mind.
Well, he's truly fed up
And he thinks it's not fair –
He can't roll on his back
With his paws in the air.
From this vast world around him
Can't somebody come
To tell him he's gorgeous –
And tickle his tum?

Irene Yates

In a Minute

A poem for two voices: a mother and a son

Mum, p-l-e-a-s-e help me do my Maths.
In a minute, son.
But I'll get told off and it's time for school!
When I've got this done.

Mum! There's a dragon in the yard!
In a minute, son.
It's green and slimy, with dead sharp claws!
When I've got this done.

Mum! It's breaking down the door!
In a minute, son.
But it's snapping its jaws and breathing fire!
When I've got this done.

Son, there's a dragon in the house!
In a minute, Mum.
It's coming to get me! Help me! H-e-l-p!
When I've got this done.

Jennifer Tweedie

To the Owner of That Dog

Dear Neighbour,

Your dog has been in my garden pond again. Really, enough is enough! Yesterday I found him swimming round and round the pond smashing the lily pads and scaring the living daylights out of my goldfish. You must keep him under control. I insist!

When he saw me he started to bark like a lunatic. I tried to grab his tail but missed. I fell into the water. I was soaked, soaked to the skin! Really, enough is enough! Next thing I know he's out of the pond and leaping the garden fence. I stood there, in the pond, with a goldfish wriggling on top of my head.

P.T.O.

Perhaps you remember the time he got into my kitchen. I'll merely remind you of the damage he did to my cornflakes, pickled onions, sausages, cheese, and cream crackers. The worst moment was when I stepped on a packet of butter he'd been chewing and went headlong under the kitchen table. Really, enough is enough!

If you don't keep that wild beast under control I'll be forced to call the police. . . or buy a large shot-gun. It's either that, or stocking the pond with a dog-eating shark! That will teach him a lesson.

Yours, in great anger,

Mr Goldfisher

Wes Magee

Letters from the Seasons

Dear Spring,

It's cold here. The weather has been terrible. It snowed for days and nobody could get out of the house. When it stopped snowing the children went out and built a huge snowman in the corner of the garden. There's still a little bit of snow left in the shade. The new baby stays in the house most of the time, and I can hear her crying.

See you soon,

Yours sincerely,
Winter

Dear Summer,

It's lovely here. The weather has been fine. It was windy last week, though, and it blew some slates off the house. When the wind dropped the children came out and played in the garden. They've got a sandpit, it's a huge one, and they keep it in the corner by the hedge. The baby sometimes comes out and lies in her pram, and I can hear her laughing.

See you soon,

All the best,
Spring

Dear Autumn,

It's hot here. The weather has been lovely. It was so hot last week that some people stayed in the house, where it was cooler. The children came out and played in their paddling pool. It's a huge one, and they've moved the sandpit to fit it in the corner of the garden. The baby sits outside all the time, and I can hear her trying to talk.

See you soon,

Keep smiling,
Summer

Dear Winter,

It's cool here. The weather has been changing. It's dark in the evenings and the children stay inside. They did come out one evening last week and built a huge bonfire in the corner of the garden where the paddling pool used to be. I see the baby in the house, trying to walk, holding on to furniture.

Don't forget to wrap up warm,

Look after yourself,

See you soon,
Autumn

Ian McMillan

OXFORD
UNIVERSITY PRESS

Great Clarendon Street, Oxford OX2 6DP

Oxford University Press is a department of the University of Oxford.
It furthers the University's objective of excellence in research, scholarship,
and education by publishing worldwide in

Oxford New York

Athens Auckland Bangkok Bogotá Buenos Aires Calcutta
Cape Town Chennai Dar es Salaam Delhi Florence Hong Kong Istanbul
Karachi Kuala Lumpur Madrid Melbourne Mexico City Mumbai
Nairobi Paris São Paulo Singapore Taipei Tokyo Toronto Warsaw

and associated companies in Berlin Ibadan

Oxford is a trade mark of Oxford University Press
in the UK and in certain other countries

© Oxford University Press 2000
First published 2000

British Library Cataloguing in publication Data
Data available

ISBN 0 19834195 4

Also available as a Big Book
Texts for Sharing 1 Big Book ISBN 0 19834196 2

Printed in Hong Kong

Acknowledgements

The Editor and Publisher are grateful for permission to reprint the
following copyright material:

Dave Calder: 'Snake's Dance' from *Bamboozled* (Other Publications, 1987) and
'Pants', © Dave Calder 1998, first published in John Foster (Ed): *Word Whirls*
(OUP, 1998), reprinted by permission of the author; Ann Cameron: 'The Pudding
Like a Night on the Sea' from *The Julian Stories*, reprinted by permission of
Victor Gollancz Ltd; John Cotton: 'Orange' and 'Pineapple', both © John Cotton
1998, first published in John Foster (Ed): *Word Whirls* (OUP, 1998), reprinted by
permission of the author; Stanley Cook: 'The Giant Awakes', © Stanley Cook
1992, first published in Brian Moses: *The Hamster's Diary* (OUP, 1992), reprinted
by permission of the author; Ian McMillan: 'Letter From the Seasons',
© Ian McMillan 1992, first published in Brian Moses: *The Hamster's Diary* (OUP,
1992), reprinted by permission of the Author; Wes Magee: 'To the Owner of
That Dog', © Wes Magee 1992, first published in Brian Moses: *The Hamster's
Diary* (OUP, 1992), reprinted by permission of the author; Judith Nicholls:
'Fun with Lists' ('Tens'), © Judith Nicholls 1992, first published in Brian Moses:
The Hamster's Diary (OUP, 1992), reprinted by permission of the Author;
Janis Priestley: 'Sea horses', © Janis Priestley 1998, first published in John Foster
(Ed): *Word Whirls* (OUP, 1998), reprinted by permission of the author; John Rice:
'On a Wet Sunday', © John Rice 1993, first published in John Foster: *It's My Dog*
(OUP, 1993), reprinted by permission of the author; Jennifer Tweedie:
'In a Minute', © Jennifer Tweedie 1994, first published in John Foster: *Got You,
Pirate!* (OUP, 1994), reprinted by permission of the author; Irene Yates:
'Surprise Your Mum Mocha Chocca Trifle" © Irene Yates 1992, first published in
Brian Moses: *The Hamster's Diary* (OUP, 1992); and 'Steg-in-the-Dumps',
© Irene Yates 1992, first published in John Foster: *Hammy's House* (OUP, 1992),
both reprinted by permission of the author.

The illustrations are by:

Katinka Kew   p. 2
David Pattison   p. 12
James Brown   p. 16
Diana Mayo   p. 18
Stephanie Strickland   p. 20
Jocelyn Wild   p. 22
John Crawford Fraser   p. 26

Cover by Jane Tattersfield